SING
OUT
LOUD
BOOK II
Developing Your Voice

Jaime Vendera &
Anne Loader McGee

VP
Vendera
Publishing

Vendera Publishing

Interior Design by Daniel Middleton | www.scribefreelance.com
Cover Design by Molly Burnside | www.crosssidedesigns.com
Photo detail: Abby Hunter and Tommie Armstrong
Copyright © 2011 by Kevin Hoops | Impressive Studios
Pencil Drawings by Valerie Bastien
Audio examples recorded by Jaime Vendera

ISBN: 978-1-936307-09-8

Published in the United States of America

Books by Jaime Vendera

*Raise Your Voice Second Edition
*The Ultimate Breathing Workout
*The Ultimate Vocal Workout Diary
*Voice RX
*Vocal RESET
*Extreme Scream series
*Online Teaching Secret Revealed
*Unleash Your Creative Mindset

Books by Anne McGee

*Strengthening Your Singing Voice (Elizabeth Sabine)
*The Mystery at Marlatt Manor
*Anni's Attic

Contents

Introduction

Welcome to *Sing Out Loud Book II,* the vocal training series specifically designed for YOU, the singer! We're glad to see you've made it through *Sing Out Loud Book I.* If our calculations are correct, you've spent the last month practicing a variety of exercises, which should have produced some noticeable changes in the sound of your voice.

We're sure you've developed a solid foundation of vocal basics, learned to breathe properly, maintained breath support, and placed the sound of your voice up into your palate to feel that amazing buzz. Now it's time to move forward and begin building your vocal machine.

This system is based on tried and true vocal methods that have existed for hundreds of years. They're the same techniques that have helped thousands of singers mold their voices into the perfect vocal instrument. The *Sing Out Loud* system will prepare you for the lead in a musical, the solo in a choir, a spotlight in a talent show, or get you ready to become a singer in your own pop, country, rap, or rock band.

In *Sing Out Loud Book II* we'll take a break from all of the wild and crazy sounds you've been practicing and move forward into a series of vocal building exercises and scales that can be used both as your warm-up and your workout. You won't need to learn tons of exercises because we've streamlined a vocal workout that combines the best of the best. By the time you finish this workout, it will feel as if your vocal cords have just benched-pressed a hundred pounds at the gym.

Now it's time to delve deeper into the concepts you learned in *Sing Out Loud Book I,* expanding on what you already know so you can perfect your vocal technique. But first we need to revisit your vocal technique. It may seem boring, but it's VERY important you master the *Sing Out Loud* techniques inside and out.

Think of this book as the second vocal lesson that builds on your previous vocal knowledge. Even though it will seem like a lot of repeated information, but DO NOT skip to the back of the book just to start the exercises and avoid covering the previously learned information. Once you've studied the new techniques in *Sing Out Loud Book II*, the old techniques will begin to feel like second nature.

This book demands a lot more work and attention so be prepared for tougher assignments. Don't worry though, it will still be lots of fun. Your assignments will push you to the next level by challenging you vocally, and adding new and exciting exercises to help you master the technique.

Special Note: This book comes with a series of audio files, which were created to guide you through the vocal examples in this book. All **bold** words in parenthesis refer to an accompanying audio track, which you'll find at: http://venderapublishing.com/sing-out-loud-book-two/

So, without further ado, let's get crack-a-lackin'.

Chapter 1
Who's Been Singing Out Loud?

You should recall that we told you to continue singing every day while learning the techniques in *Sing Out Loud Book I*. We hope you all listened and have been singing out loud. In this book nothing has changed. Keep doing what you've been doing, but before we move on, we do have a few questions to ask. And on that note, it looks as if it's time for your first assignment.

Assignment #1—Q & A Time

Open up another document on your computer, then write down and answer the following questions:

1) Has your singing improved since you started practicing? If so, in what way?
2) Are you noticing any changes in your voice? List the changes.
3) Since you've started studying the *Sing Out Loud* series, do you feel any more confident now when you sing, or do you still feel shy singing in front of other people?

If you struggle with the shyness factor, please be aware that these are all natural feelings. It simply indicates a lack of self-confidence and can be overcome. *Sing Out Loud Book II* will teach you how to let go of these feelings. You CAN sing, you CAN sing well, and you CAN easily sing in front of other people. For those of you who are doubtful about how well you sing, or for those still too scared to even try, think on this:

**If you can speak, then with a little training,
you can learn how to sing—and sing well!**

Remember, singing is nothing more than drawn-out speech. It doesn't matter if you don't yet sound like a rock star, you will find YOUR rock star sound soon. As long as you faithfully practice these techniques and exercises and express the music and words of your song with feeling and passion, we guarantee you'll soon discover the ability to capture an audience.

Broken record time... Before jumping into *Sing Out Loud Book II*, let's recap the *Sing Out Loud* golden rule.

If it hurts to sing, you are doing something wrong!

Since you are familiar with the instructions in *Sing Out Loud Book I*, some of the following information won't be news to you. If you haven't read the first book in the series, then you might end up a little confused. We suggest you read *Sing Out Loud Book I* before going any further. Repeating and drilling the basic concepts into your brain is the only way to make sure you get the technique down, and because these techniques will be used for the rest of your life, it's important to master them now.

To repeat, if at any time while singing or doing the exercises, your voice begins to hurt, you must stop immediately. It could simply be that you are straining and need a slight vocal adjustment. It's important to focus on singing correctly from the very start. That way you won't ever have this problem. Also, keep in mind there may be times when your throat muscles feel a little sore. This is normal. You are building strength in the muscles of the neck, throat, chin, stomach, diaphragm, back, and between your ribcage (intercostals muscles). Slight soreness is to be expected. But there is a HUGE difference between pain from vocal abuse and pain from building the voice.

If you experience any slight soreness in your muscles during an exercise, take a five-minute mini-break, and then try the exercise again. If it's soreness from muscle building, the pain will subside quickly. If it's pain from strain, it will be painful and your voice will tire quickly. It will even cause you to become husky and lose range. If this happens, simply stop the exercise and take a quick break before moving on to the next exercise. Strain is a sign that you're trying to push past your current limits. DO NOT force your voice to go higher on the exercises. It will only slow your progress. With time, you will build up your vocal muscles and be able to reach those higher notes.

Even though the techniques in the *Sing Out Loud* books are designed to prevent strain from happening, you still must use common sense. Let your voice be your guide, and learn to take a break when your voice tells you it needs one. Now, if you're ready to rock, let's get to it.

Chapter 2
Singing — It's All in Your Head

Everyone is born to sing, but as we have all heard, there are people who naturally sound better than others, just as there are people who are naturally gifted at playing sports. Does that mean you cannot become a good singer? Absolutely not! If you can sustain a word, you can learn to sing.

The first thing you should understand before sustaining that first word is that singing is 90% mental. How you think and feel about your voice will affect how you sound. So to get started on the right track, begin mentally "hearing" your voice in your head before you actually start to sing. Singing should begin as a *thought* in your mind before you open your mouth, and it should remain in your mind after you close your mouth. It's the job of your vocal cords and body to remember that sound.

On that note it looks like it's time for another assignment.

Assignment #2—The Voice of the Mind

One of the best ways to learn a song is to listen to the song over and over again while you sing along with it in your mind. So, jumping back to *Sing Out Loud Book I*, pull out the original copy of your *Sing Out Loud* practice song; the song you sang and recorded at the beginning of this series. Now you'll take that song to the next level by listening to it all day today. Your goal is to listen to it fifty times.

You might think that listening to a song that many times in a day will take forever, but if your song is less than four minutes long, it will take less than three and a half hours to finish this assignment. Hey, we're sure you've watched a movie or played video games for longer than three-hours, so live it, love it, do it! We told you this book was going to be a lot tougher, so bottom line, if you want to sing, you must be willing to put in the time.

While listening to your song, alternate between listening to the song once, and then singing it in your head the next time it plays. As you mentally sing along, listen for your voice. *Hear* how you would sing the song. You don't want to become a singing clone; you want to hear the song in your head with YOUR voice. So listen intently on the odd-numbered plays and sing along mentally on the even-numbered plays, listening specifically for your own sound.

It's also important that you pay attention to your vocal technique as you mentally sing along to the song. Physically go through the actual movements, even though you aren't producing any sound with your voice. Take a breath where the singer takes a breath, expand your belly, back and ribs, and push down the same way we've instructed you to do. You should also articulate the words with your mouth. So, on with your next assignment.

Assignment #3—It's Time to Record Yourself . . . Again!

Now you'll re-record your practice song. Grab the old recording device and in one take, give it your best shot. Warm-up your voice first with some lip bubbles, then sing your heart out in one take. Label and save the audio file to your *Sing Out Loud* practice folder.

Assignment #4—Let's Compare

Hold up, wild child, you aren't finished yet. Now it's time to do side-by-side comparisons. Play the very first version you recorded way back in *Sing Out Loud Book I* and then listen to your newest recording. It's time to expand your notes. Pop open your word processor and create a brand new likes/dislikes file. Write down any and all vocal differences between the two versions. Note differences like "version two sounded more in tune than the first" one, or "my breathing was more consistent on the second recording", or "my voice sounds stronger now". These are very important details. If there were things you liked better about the first recording, make a note of those as well. Sometimes singers will do things vocally even on a so-so recording that can sound really cool. Maybe you did a cool vocal lick on the first recording. That's something you'll want to remember, because the cool things should be added to your "vocal bag of tricks" to be used later when you sing other songs.

Assignment #5—Critique Time

Now that you've compared the two recordings, it's time to let someone else listen to the new version so you can get a true critique of your voice and your progress. A music teacher or choir director would be your best bet for an honest critique. Sometimes it's tough to let friends or parents listen because the critiques may be biased by their feelings. Your parents may say it sounds amazing, or a friend may say it stinks. Every parent thinks their son or daughter is the next big superstar vocalist, and friends can be cruel if that old jealousy bug creeps in. An incorrect critique won't help you to progress vocally, whether it's a good one or a bad one. You need to know what you are doing right or wrong, so you can improve. Don't be influenced by the wrong information about your voice.

Find someone who understands music and will listen with honest ears. When you receive that critique, you must consider their criticism with an open mind. Whether you get a positive or negative critique, don't get a big ego, or let your feelings become bruised. Take their comments or suggestions like a professional and use it to improve your singing. If someone says you're flat on the chorus, instead of getting upset, work on the chorus until you can sing it correctly. Okay, enough with the assignments, back to studying.

Once you've become motivated to practice the *Sing Out Loud* exercises, you will begin building the strength needed for a top-notch instrument, but again, watch that your emotions stay upbeat because your mood will affect your voice. Hurtful emotions make the voice constrict, while happy emotions free the voice and allow you to sing with freedom. We bet you can't remember one time when you lost your voice from laughing. That's because your voice works better when you're happy.

Just so we're clear, you don't need to be sad to express extremely painful emotions when you sing. Negative emotions will take over your voice if you're truly upset so put your practice on hold for a few hours until you feel better. It's important to laugh a lot and stay happy.

Now that you're happy and giggling like a lunatic, let's jump back to the vocal cords. Vocal cord vibration must continue from word to word, pitch-to-pitch, and even held mentally over the silent parts of a song in order to maintain that mind/body connection. Remember, the mind and body work together subconsciously whenever you sing. You should not have to think about how you say or see a word. Just open your mouth and do it and your mind will work with the muscles to produce the desired result.

Think back to the second assignment in this book. If you sang that song right now, you'd notice it would float right out of you and the words would be there before you even knew it. It's as if the song had been imprinted on your mind. Trust us, it has been.

Since you now know that singing is both physical and mental, you can say that the two main components of singing consist of sustained speech and mentally "hearing" your voice. Great singers say they can *hear* their entire song in advance, as though it's coming from their imagination. How can this be? Well, it's because they've practiced their material over and over until they know it so well they could sing the song, note for note, line for line, even without the music. But it takes more than just memorizing a song in order to sing like a professional. The following is a list of five points you must master to become a GREAT singer:

1) **Correct Breathing & Support**

   If you intend to become a great singer, you MUST master your breathing. This includes both inhaling and exhaling. Thanks to our instruction in *Sing Out Loud Book I*, you are well on your way. Mastering your breathing adds power and protects the voice from vocal blowout (strain). Many singers will find that vocal blowout is generally related to using too much air. The *Sing Out Loud* approach to minimal air pressure prevents vocal loss.

   Believe it or not, the ability to use very little breath begins with tightening the stomach. Tightening the stomach for breath support is all about developing the ability to control the release of the breath and delivering the right amount of air to maintain each note and phrase.

   To sing well, air pressure must be balanced. Remember, if you use too little breath, you'll never make it to the end of a phrase and risk going flat, and if you use too much air, your pitch may go sharp.

Sing Out Loud students ALWAYS sing fuel-efficient and strain free.

2) Catching the "Buzz" of Resonance

Remember in *Sing Out Loud Book I* the example of the kid brother or sister bouncing off the walls after drinking all that soda? Or the leaky hose nozzle that let water go flying all over the place? By catching the buzz, you'll focus the voice so you'll never lose vocal energy, and by focusing the spinning vibration of your voice up into the soft palate, you'll combine the palate buzz with the body buzz. This is the secret to great tone and vocal freedom.

3) Enunciation

Enunciation is very important if you want to become known as a GREAT singer. Make your words clear or the tone will sound as if it's stuck in the back of your throat—another way to end up with vocal strain. Trapped energy can also cause physical problems in the throat. You remember that nasty word "nodule" don't you? Let's not go that route. Open your mouth wide enough to get the words out clearly and distinctly. This is a major part of singing correctly.

"But how can I tell if I'm mumbling and the sound is trapped in the back of my throat?"

We'll answer your question with a question of our own. "Can people understand the lyrics when you sing them?"

If you sound like the Ham Burglar when you sing, you'll simply drive fans away. There's no point in sounding great melodically if no one can understand your words. The audience may have paid good money to come to your show so be prepared to give them what they've paid for. Keep the tongue down, the jaw dropped, and the mouth open. And now, to help develop your enunciation, we're giving you another assignment.

Assignment #6—Mastering the Mumbles

If you've been told you mumble, don't fret because it's easily corrected. Listen back to your recordings paying close attention to your enunciation.

Could you understand every word you were singing? Write down each word you didn't understand. Once you know the problem words, practice over-pronouncing each one ten times. Once you've worked through your list, go back and recite the words to the *entire* song out loud, slowly and clearly, over-enunciating all the lyrics. Once you feel you can speak each word clearly, re-record the song again and make sure you've mastered the mumbles.

4) Vocal Development

Every time you practice and sing, you should feel as if you are using every muscle in your body. It's important to work these muscles daily. We can't emphasize enough that the more you apply the *Sing Out Loud* vocal techniques and do the vocal exercises, the stronger your voice will become and the more you will feel like a well-tuned instrument.

5) Emotional Expression

Who wants to hear a BORING singer? Absolutely no one! Remember how we asked you in *Sing Out Loud Book I* to mimic the sounds with enthusiasm, pretending to become the animal or baby you were imitating? Well the reason is because we wanted you to *feel* the emotion associated with each sound.

Keep in mind that singing is an art form and YOU are the artist. Adding emotion and feeling to your voice makes singing exciting. When you sing with emotion you don't just sustain words, you paint a believable picture. By making changes in dynamics (from soft to loud), adjusting tonal colors (from dark to bright), changing tonal types (from falsetto to full voice), and mixing up your phrases (from fast choppy words to long drawn out ones), you can create a beautiful tapestry that will tell a story in your song.

Bottom line is, it's your job to use a palette of emotions to make listeners believe the words you are singing. Vocally paint a beautiful picture that your listeners can *see* with their ears. The audience should know when you're either angry, sad, happy, jealous, excited, or scared.

These five steps will be discussed in more detail throughout the *Sing Out Loud* series. If it's confusing at this point, don't worry, you'll understand in time. Meantime we'll revisit the basics of the *Sing Out Loud* vocal technique, so let's mosey on over to the next chapter and get started.

Chapter 3
A Refresher Course

The *Sing Out Loud* technique is broken down as follows:

> ➢ Secret Step #1:   Breathe in
> ➢ Secret Step #2:   Add support
> ➢ Secret Step #3:   Feel the buzz

#1—Breathe In
Inhale quietly on a yawn right before you sing. Fill your tank from the bottom up and expand out your belly, back, and ribs. Take in just the right amount of breath needed for each phrase you sing.

#2—Add Support
Add energy to your voice using minimal air release while pushing down like you're going to the bathroom. Tighten your stomach muscles each time you speak or sing. Not only do tight stomach muscles support your voice, they also give you power, and as you already know, power is energy.

#3—Feel The Buzz
Buzz is the sensation of resonance vibrating in the roof of the mouth (palate) and in various parts of the body. The buzz will occur in many different places, such as the chest for low notes and the head for high notes. But the one place you must always feel the buzz is in the roof of your mouth.

New paragraph. The buzz will occur naturally when you apply the first two steps. By feeling the buzz, you'll know you're breathing, supporting, and singing correctly and this will keep you from straining your voice. The palate buzz corrects the leaky nozzle problem and allows you to correctly focus the energy produced by the vocal cords.

In reality, you should consider your whole body as a *buzzing* instrument. If you play a saxophone, the vibration of the sound made from the reed can be felt in every part of the instrument. Everything vibrates, from your instrument to a glass of water. Don't believe us? See if your mom has a fine collection of crystal wine glasses. Flick the side of one with your finger and listen to the pitch it makes. Now sing that exact pitch next to the glass and watch the glass vibrate in tune with your voice.

Whenever you produce sound, different parts of your body will vibrate to the different pitches. That's why you'll feel more chest vibration on low notes and more head vibration on high notes. As we mentioned in *Sing out Loud Book I*, you are a giant tuning fork that vibrates to the sound of your voice. The more your tuning fork vibrates, the better you'll sound.

As you may recall, when you inhale you fill your lungs up with air, this air becomes your vocal fuel. You then add the "power" that helps move this fuel up and out by turning on your power generator or amplifier (the diaphragm) and tightening your abdominal muscles. The power generator then delivers your fuel (air) through your vocal cords, up the windpipe (trachea), and into your sinus cavities where it's released out through your mouth. In other words, this tiny release of air, which begins in the lungs and is controlled by the diaphragm, turns into sound at the vocal cords and is converted into words as it flows out through the mouth. This release from within the body is known as the "vocal path".

We said earlier that when your vocal fuel (air) is released, the vocal cords begin to open and close at a rapid, repetitive rate as they automatically try to resist the air pressure. This continual cycle of opening and closing of the cords when air passes through them produces a vibration. It is this vibration that converts the fuel into sound. And don't forget, not only does your throat help form the words, but also your sinuses, jaw, teeth, lips and tongue. This adds color to the sounds when you sing.

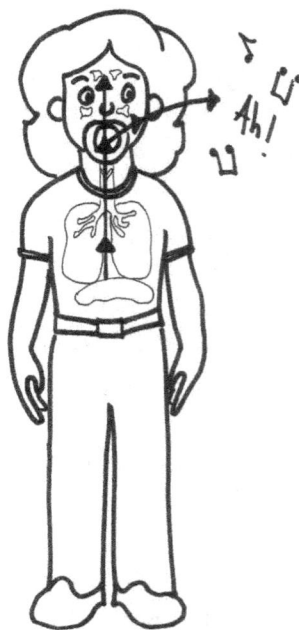

20

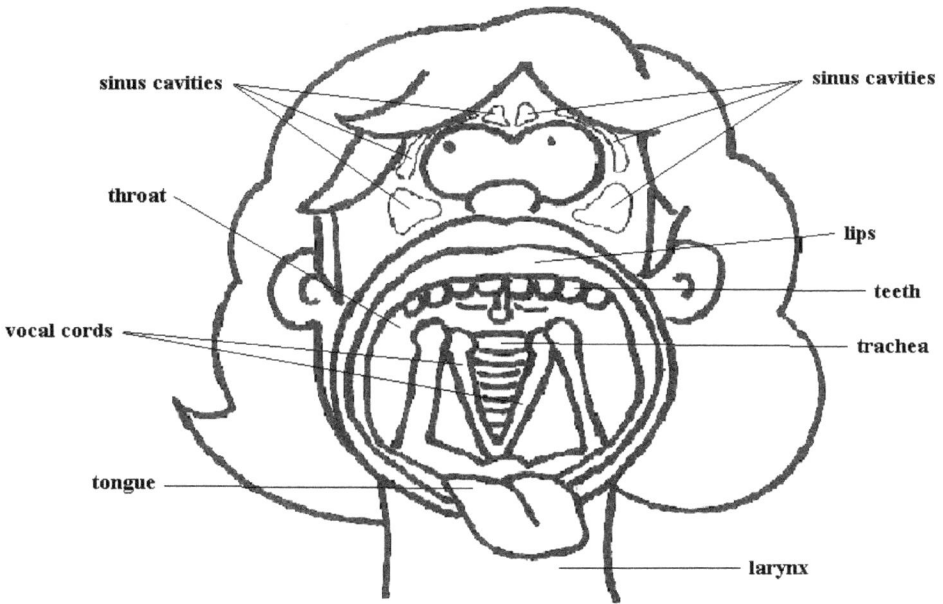

When you fully understand the concepts presented in this chapter, we guarantee you'll unleash vocal power such as you've never known before. At this point though, we want you to take a small break and think about what you've learned so far. When you're ready to proceed, we'll build upon what you already know.

Chapter 4
Freeing the Vocal Cords

Before we delve further, however, we should revisit the vocal cords. These little frequency generators are definitely one of God's amazing creations. They are approximately a quarter to a half-inch in length and simply by vibrating together, can produce a variety of frequencies that ultimately turn into glorious sounds.

As you know, the vocal cords are in the larynx, that protruding bump on the front of your throat known as the Adam's apple. Many singers have trouble with the larynx rising up when singing high notes. If this sounds like a problem you might have, you want to nip this in the bud immediately. Allowing the larynx to rise when singing is like folding a hose in half to prevent water from being released—the pressure builds up and can cause the hose to burst. For singers, this means you're creating a blockage of your vocal fuel or energy release, which could cause strain and/or vocal damage.

A high larynx will make your voice sound thin and weak, and sometimes nasally. On the other hand if the larynx drops too low, such as when taking a big yawn, you'll sound as if you're doing voice-overs for a cartoon soundtrack. While a lower larynx doesn't cause as much strain as a higher larynx, it can still alter your tone. (**Swallowing and yawning voice**)

The larynx should only move up or down slightly as you sing. This slight up and down movement doesn't affect the pitch, but it does affect the tonal quality. The best position for the larynx is in a relaxed neutral position.

Assignment #7—Larynx Control

Since the larynx seems to have a mind of its own, this assignment is designed to teach you how to control an unruly larynx. Look in a mirror and while sustaining a note, slide up in range as high as you can comfortably go without straining. You'll reach a point where the larynx will start to rise up in the throat and the tone of your voice will begin to go thin. If possible, note the actual pitch where your larynx becomes a nuisance. If you have a guitar or keyboard, it should be easy to find the exact musical note.

Repeat the slide, while placing your hand on your larynx like our friend Tommie Armstrong is doing in the picture to the right. As you slide up in pitch and the larynx begins to move, gently apply a bit of downward pressure with your hand, as if telling your larynx to stand back.

Your goal isn't to force the larynx down; it's to create a slight opposition so that your mind begins to work with your muscles to stop the larynx from rising up and cutting off your vocal energy path. Many singers face this problem and it can be the root of all vocal strain for many. As you begin practicing the vocal scales in this book, the hand-on-the-larynx-technique will become an invaluable tool in teaching the muscles of your throat not to rise up as you go for higher notes.

Think back to the rubber band analogy from *Sing Out Loud Book I*. Placing strain on your voice as you climb higher in pitch is like stretching a rubber band beyond its elasticity point. This will only cause it to break. You don't want to "snap" your vocal cords, so don't stretch them beyond your current limit. You'll prevent this from ever happening if you apply correct breath technique, support, and buzz, along with training your larynx to relax.

Bad technique and a high larynx leads to vocal damage, such as a hoarse voice, or worse, vocal nodules or rupture of the vocal cords. What are nodules? They are calluses on the vocal cords, similar to the calluses a guitar player develops on his fingers from picking guitar strings. Guitar players welcome calluses because the thickened skin on their fingers allows them to play for longer periods of time without cutting their fingers sliding on the metal strings.

But calluses don't benefit singers as they do guitarists. A nodule on the vocal cords can turn a great singing tone into a nasty, husky tone with limited range. This could ultimately end a singer's career. Nodules can be

removed by surgery, but there's a risk the voice may not fully recover.

Calluses aren't the only problems singers can face. When we abuse our voice, the vocal cords become dry, inflamed and irritated, and may lead to swollen blood vessels. These swollen blood vessels can turn into blisters, which are also known as polyps. A polyp appears when the tiny capillaries on the mucosa (the surface tissue of the vocal cords) burst. Usually busted capillaries will self-repair, but if the abuse continues and polyps appear, it often results in surgery.

Both nodules and polyps affect vocal cord vibration and the overall sound of the voice. If you cannot produce vibration through the normal opening and closing action of the vocal cords, then you won't be able to produce a sustained note. In a normal situation when the air supply vibrates the vocal cords, a clear sound is produced. If the cords cannot completely seal because of a nodule or polyp, the sound quality produces a breathy, husky, or choppy sound, noticeable as a huge break in your voice. Depending on the damage, you may not even be able to speak. If you master the *Sing Out Loud* techniques and work through the assignments and exercises, we can almost guarantee you'll never have to worry about vocal damage.

Now it's time for a breathing refresher course to see how well you are progressing—oxygen-wise.

Chapter 5
How's Your Breathing

In the following four steps we'll break down how you should breathe:

1. Inhale silently on a slight yawn and take in a cupful of air
2. Fill the lungs from the bottom-up
3. Allow the belly, back, and ribs to expand outward
4. Keep the shoulders and chest relaxed

That sums it up. See you next chapter... Just teasing! It's time to take your breathing exercises to the next level. Your breath is the core of the *Sing Out Loud* system. It gives you power, allows you to sustain notes, plays a partial role in controlling your volume, and most importantly, keeps you from vocal burnout.

In the late 1800s, which was considered by many to be the Golden Age of music and song, the renowned vocal teacher, Giovanni Battista Lamperti once said:

Great singers must be able to compress the breath, hold it firmly with the abdomen, gauge its use with the diaphragm, turn it into vibration with the throat, and make it bloom at the lips as tone.

Those are powerful words. Whenever you start singing, you should let the air do the work, not the throat muscles. Never "pull" in the air, simply allow the lungs to expand naturally by *drinking* it in. If the lungs are expanding correctly, it will feel as if you are filling up your lower body.

As you sing, the air that leaves your mouth should be pure vocal energy. It should NEVER sound breathy unless it is intentional. Some singers, such as John Mayer, often sing breathy. This is to create a smoky tone for a vocal effect. Singing breathy so you can add color to your song is fine, but when you practice vocal exercises, your tone must be clean and clear on every single note. If you tone is not pure then you are doing something wrong.

Many times the tone might not be clear because of a singer's attempt to control the sound from the throat. If the larynx is rising up or if you squeeze in the throat, like grunting, it will make your tone thin and/or scratchy. Some other reasons your voice may not sound clear is lack of hydration, using too much breath, or drying your vocal cords out while inhaling. If you follow the techniques you learned in *Sing Out Loud Book I*, none of these reasons should apply to you. However, sometimes the voice can become dry from vocal practice so a good tip is to breathe in through your nose to help moisten the vocal cords.

This last tip may leave you wondering if you should inhale through your nose or mouth all the time. Breathing through the nose moistens the air because the sinus passages are always moist. Since the vocal cords must stay lubricated to work efficiently, then breathing through the nose might be your best bet. Although many singers choose to breathe through the mouth when they sing, others alternate, breathing through the mouth throughout most of their song and only breathing through the nose during a guitar solo, or in the quick break before the chorus. The correct answer is, do whatever feels right. But we might suggest you use nostril breathing if your voice feels dry.

With that said, let's review how to take the proper breath. The first thing is to stop chest breathing. If the chest expands out and the shoulders lift up as if you're getting ready for a fight, you add tension to your neck, which creates throat tension. Tommie is demonstrating the chest breathing position in the picture to the right. If you look like this when you breathe, you're on the wrong track. The correct way is to breathe low into the body. This has been known for centuries as diaphragmatic breathing, which occurs when the diaphragm expands downward, causing the belly, back, and ribs to expand outwards.

Assignment #8—Expanding the Ribs

To help you understand this concept, let's go back to the analogy of the water balloon, which automatically fills from the bottom up. Think of your lungs as doing the same thing. Place your hands on your sides as you inhale. Your hands should kick outwards without lifting your shoulders. This is easily accomplished when you visualize filling the lungs at the bottom first. If you feel like you'll need more breath, you *can* expand the chest. In fact, chest expansion is fine, as long as it's the *last* thing you do. You don't want the chest to expand before any other body part. You want to feel as if you're drinking in air, all the way down to below your belly button, then filling from that point up. As long as your belly expands out without any forced effort and your hands kick out to your sides, you'll know you're doing it right. So place your hands on your sides like Tommie is doing in the picture to the right, take in ten deep breaths and allow the hands to lift out as the ribs expand. Tommie's hands are at the very bottom of his rib cage. You may have to bring the hands a bit higher to feel the full expansion. If you're having trouble making this happen, try the following exercises and it will soon become second nature.

Assignment #9—More Breathing Exercises

And you thought you were done with these breathing exercises in *Sing Out Loud Book I*. You naïve singer, now it's time for the real work.

Breathing Exercise 1—Belly Expansion

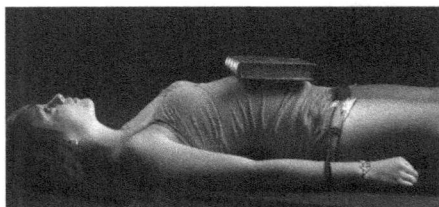

INHALE—BOOK UP   **EXHALE—BOOK DOWN**

For this exercise, you need to lie on the floor and place a heavy book on top of your stomach. Once you are comfortable, take a slow deep breath. The book should rise up as you inhale, like our friend Abby Hunter is doing in the picture on the left. Next, exhale and allow the book to drop back to its starting position until your stomach flattens like Abby's.

Now that you're accustomed to this exercise, it's time for some more serious breath work. While still lying on your back with the book on your stomach, inhale with an open mouth as quickly and as deeply as you can, then force every ounce of air out of your lungs in one expulsion of breath. Repeat this exercise fifty times in a row. This may make you feel warm and tingly all over, and possibly even a little dizzy. It's the result of an increase of fresh oxygen in your body.

Once you've finished your fifty breaths, immediately stand up and repeat this exercise using your hand on your stomach in place of the book. Do fifty more big breaths. It might help if you lean up against a wall while doing this exercise. We don't want you passing out and falling backwards. If you feel light headed before you finish, you should stop and take a break.

EXHALE—HAND IN   **EXHALE—HAND OUT**

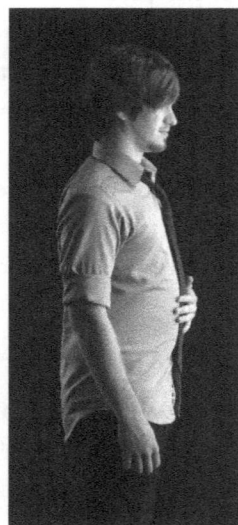

Breathing Exercise 2—The Super Hiss

This is simply a repeat of the hissing exercise from *Sing Out Loud Book I*. It can be done either lying down or standing up. Take a deep breath and forcefully hiss out every last ounce of air until you feel your stomach muscles begin to ache. Repeat this exercise twenty-five times in a row. After you've finished your round of super hisses, grab your timer and sustain an "aaahh" sound. It doesn't matter what note, just sustain any comfortable audible pitch. You only get one shot at this so hang on to that note as if your life depended on it. After you start to time yourself, your goal is to be able to gain one second longer each day. If you held out the note for fifteen seconds today, you want to try for sixteen seconds tomorrow, seventeen the day after . . . you get the picture. (**The Super Hiss**)

Breathing Exercise 3—Start Counting

Count as high as you can on one breath, making sure to speak slowly and clearly. Repeat this exercise ten times per day. (**Start Counting**)

Breathing Exercise 4—The Balloon Exercise Revisited

Surely you remember all the fun you had blowing up balloons in *Sing Out Loud Book I?* Well it's time to take it up a notch. Buy a pack of fifty balloons, lay them out on a table, turn on your timer and see how quickly you can blow up all fifty. This isn't as easy as it sounds. Once you blow up a balloon you must tie it and throw it to one side. But wait, it gets harder. While you're tying the balloon, pant like a dog until you start blowing up the next balloon. If you need to take a few seconds to yawn, catch your breath, or take a sip of water, then do so, but try to keep it going without these breaks if you can.

These exercises will replace the breathing exercises from *Sing Out Loud Book I*. Begin practicing these new breathing exercises immediately, five times per week, with the exception of the balloon exercise. It only needs to be performed on the fifth day. It's more of a test to check your breathing progress. If you've worked through the new breathing set today, we're proud of you. Take the rest of the day off and we'll see you tomorrow in the next chapter.

Chapter 6
Blasting Your Speaker Box

We all know that the secret to turning on your speaker is by tightening the abdominal muscles. Now it's time to learn how to better control that speaker and add more volume without blowing out your throat. It all occurs by simply adjusting your breath support.

An easy way to remember how to adjust breath support is to think of a car or go-kart. You have to put your foot on the gas pedal and push down in order to make the car move ahead, otherwise you'll just sit there. To go a little faster, you push down harder and give it more gas. To stay at your desired speed, you must keep the same consistent pressure on the gas pedal. When you want to slow down, you let your foot off the pedal. Of course, if you take your foot completely off the pedal it will cause the car to eventually roll to a stop.

Just like putting your foot down on the gas pedal, in order to create more abdominal pressure you have to push down like going to the toilet. To sing higher with ease and without strain, add more downward pressure. In other words, give it more gas. Once you've reached your desired singing note, then it's important to maintain that same kind of pressure. To sing lower, let up on your abdominal pressure, but not completely. That would be like lifting your foot off the gas pedal and bringing the car to a stop.

If you let go of your support when you're singing, you won't be able to feed your vocal cords adequate fuel and this will cause you to strain when reaching for the notes. So begin thinking of breath support as less pressure for low notes and more pressure for high notes. Your foot should always be ON the gas pedal when speaking or singing, and OFF the gas pedal when you're not speaking or singing.

When you sing, the downward support will vary because your melodic notes will vary in range. This doesn't mean you have to be constantly changing the pressure—just adjust it as you feel the need. You'll gradually learn how to add or subtract as needed, but don't forget, the key to the right amount of support is the buzzing sensation felt in the roof of the mouth.

Maintain that buzz and the breath support will adjust accordingly.

Now here are two important points to keep in mind:

1. If your voice sounds like it's losing volume or feels as if it's losing vocal strength, it means you've taken your foot off the gas pedal; in other words, you've quit pushing down and lost your power.

2. Going breathy when you sing means the diaphragm is relaxing too quickly. This can happen from too little support, or from supporting incorrectly. For instance, if you suck in your stomach as opposed to pushing down, it will force the diaphragm to relax. If you are breathy, it's also a sign the vocal cords have become lazy and are opening a little too wide. This is something you don't want, as it will allow air a free pass to rush out the door.

Never lose focus on your breath support. You must maintain the right amount of abdominal pressure or you won't be able to keep the air flowing up through the vocal cords. Got the hang of it? Let's do a quick review before moving on to another assignment. In actuality, the entire breathing machine can be summed up in two steps:

Step One: drink in air by opening the throat on a slight yawn and fill the tank from the bottom up, which will cause your belly, back and ribs to expand outwards.

Step Two: bear down as if you are going to the toilet. If done correctly, your stomach muscles will tighten and the diaphragm will be ready to resist the air release. Add more or less gas as needed.

These two steps MUST happen before any sound leaves your mouth. This creates your power source, which is turned into vocal energy once it passes out through the vocal cords. In other words, Step One inserts the fuel to run the machine (fills up your gas tank), and Step Two turns that fuel into power (lets you drive the car by stepping on the gas pedal). These two steps will send the vibration of your voice spinning right up into the roof of your mouth, freeing your sound. Now it's time for another assignment.

Assignment #10—Power Exercises

Just to make sure you know exactly how to put the "pedal to the metal", let's try some sounds.

Power Exercise 1—Hut Hut Hike

Have you ever played football? The Quarterback gets ready for the play and says "Hut, Hut HIKE!" He makes this sound with much power and authority. Let's give it a try. Slam the gas pedal to the floor and push down as hard as you can on every word to rev up your motor.

Say the word "Hut" as you push down, then "Hut" as you push down again, ending with "HIKE" for the third and final push. Yes, you should relax your stomach muscles between each word. If the exercise is done correctly, it will feel like each word is exploding right through the roof of your mouth. Hopefully you gained enough decibels to explode a wineglass on the TV show MythBusters. **(Hut Hut Hike)**

NOTE: This is NOT about shouting. It's about the proper release of vocal energy, which builds up resonance, which is then heard as an increase in volume.

Power Exercise 2—The E Scream

Now let's put that power to the test. Inhale, but do not tighten your stomach, just tense down slightly to feel the downward sensation. Start singing "eeeee" like in the word "sweet". Start the sound in high falsetto with a very soft volume, then as you begin to push down and add more gas, allow the sound to swell in volume and grow bigger and brighter. This sound will grow to deafening levels and you will feel the spinning vibration growing in your palate as well as throughout your body, especially your head. If it starts to hurt your throat, then you aren't focusing the tone into the roof of your mouth enough. **(The E Scream)**

Repeat this exercise at least ten times a day. It's more fun if you make this exercise a game, and even though it may drive your friends nuts, do it throughout the whole day. Before long the voice will feel stronger, brighter and cleaner with each practice. Although this exercise is performed entirely in falsetto, it's great for expanding the vocal range of your full voice. But this is enough work to help you master your speaker box. Now it's time for more buzzing.

Chapter 7
The BUZZZZZZZ

Now that we've revisited breathing and your amplification system, this is the point where you transform all that power into something you can *really* use. Time to make that car engine go VROOOOMMM! Time to get back to buzzin'. Remember, the buzz occurs simultaneously in both the palate and the entire body. Low notes give more buzz in the chest and high notes produce more buzz in the head, but palate buzz is the secret to vocal freedom. By feeling the buzz in the roof of the mouth, you'll know your machine has successfully taken the fuel, turned it into power, and transformed it into vocal energy. When this energy is "placed" in the palate with proper support, it's oftentimes called *vocal placement*. Sounds like the perfect time for another assignment.

Assignment #11—Mastering Vocal Placement

You have to maintain vocal placement in the roof of your mouth at all times in order to sing freely and sing your best. As mentioned before, the roof of the mouth is the true place where tone begins. Focusing on the palate as opposed to thinking about the vocal cords in the throat will assist you in eliminating vocal strain. The following exercises will help you latch onto correct vocal placement.

Placement Exercise 1— "Nnnggg"

If you are having trouble maintaining the vibration in the roof of your mouth, try sustaining an "nnnggg", as in the word "England" and you should begin to feel the strong vibration. It will not only vibrate in the soft palate but also vibrate in the hard part of the palate, as well. You can find the hard part of the palate by placing the tip of the tongue against the roof of the mouth at the hard palate ridge. That's the hard line inside your mouth toward the front. Say the word "Nancy". The place where your tongue touched the roof of the mouth at the start of the word is the spot where you should keep your tongue during this exercise. If your tongue vibrates or tickles when sustaining an "nnnggg" sound, you're doing it right. (**Nnnggg**)

Placement Exercise 2—The Cold Spot

A helpful trick in finding the cold spot is to take a super quick breath while yawning. You'll feel a cold spot at the back of the roof of your mouth. This "spot" is part of your "tone generator". Spin your vibration into the tone generator for effortless sound. In actuality you may feel the vibrations a little forward in the mouth as opposed to far back, and that should be your guide. If the spinning vibration falls behind or below that cold spot, then it's too far back in the throat and may be causing vocal tension. But if it's on the cold spot then you're placing your tone correctly. (**The Cold Spot**)

Once you've mastered the correct placement, it will free the voice from the constraints of the throat and increase resonance and energy for a much bigger and more pleasing sound. You'll also feel your cheeks and nose vibrate in the mask area, a sign your vocal placement is in the right place. Maintaining vocal placement, whether you're speaking or singing, is crucial to a healthy voice. If you suddenly lose your placement and the buzz is not there, try the following exercises to reestablish it.

Placement Exercise 3—Resetting Your Placement

Stand with feet slightly apart and bend over at the waist, allowing your head and hands to hang toward the ground. Begin humming until you feel vibration in the mask. This will help bring the sound up and out of the throat and place it firmly back into the palate. Immediately stand up straight while continuing to hum. You should still feel the buzzing in the mask. Switch from humming to a few good, hearty laughs and the sensation of your palate placement will return to you. Make sure you're breathing and supporting correctly as this might be the

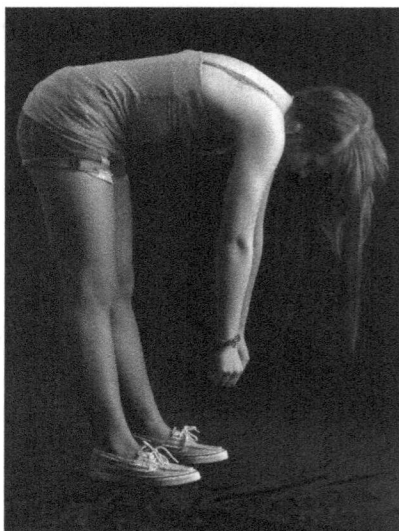

reason why you've lost that placement. Trust us, by combining proper breathing with support for power and placement, you'll turn your entire body into a singing powerhouse with enough vocal energy to light up New York City!

Psst—CONGRATULATIONS, we know this review has been tough on you, and most likely, a bit boring, but it's important you understand fully how to master the *Sing Out Loud* techniques. If you've made it this far, you're on your way to becoming a technique-savvy singer. But hold on to your shorts. We still need to build your voice with some killer vocal exercises before you take a crack at honing your singing chops. We know you're getting anxious, but hang with us. Just a few more chapters on vocal theory and then we'll start the program.

Chapter 8
All One Voice

As you recall from *Sing Out Loud Book I*, many terms have been coined in the vocal realm including chest voice, head voice, vocal break, and falsetto, just to name a few. The purpose of the *Sing Out Loud* series isn't just to teach you terms; it's to get your voice to sound the way you want it. We won't even go into other terms such as *passagio* or *adduction,* nor will we discuss the different vocal classifications such as *Tenor, Soprano, Alto, Bass,* and *Baritone.* But if you want to learn more about terminology, check out *Raise Your Voice Second Edition* by Jaime Vendera. For right now, you only need to remember one thing. No matter the terminology, it takes the same ONE VOICE!

Whether you sing in a falsetto voice, full voice, low voice, high voice, chest voice, head voice, clean voice, breathy voice, gritty voice, quiet voice, or loud voice, it all originates from one place—your vocal cords. Our goal here is to make sure your vocal cords act as one complete instrument from the bottom of your range to the top, and we can accomplish this by making singing and practicing as fun and simple as possible. We are determined to eliminate as many terms from your vocabulary as we can so you don't become a head-case trying to learn all the inner-mechanics of singing. We've seen this happen before. Trust us, knowing that the Cricothyroid muscle tilts the thyroid forward to tense the vocal cords will NOT make it any easier to sing. Did we lose you? Don't worry, you don't need to understand it to become a better singer. All you need to understand is that the voice should be viewed as one fluid, flawless instrument from low notes to high notes with no noticeable breaks in between.

The exercises in *Sing Out Loud Book II* are range and power builders. They are designed to eliminate the vocal break between the chest and head voice. These exercises will create one fluid, flawless instrument. Forget the term *chest voice.* Replace it with *low voice,* and trade *head voice* for *high voice* because in all actuality, that's all it is.

Chest voice = Low voice = Low notes
Head voice = High voice = High notes
Break point = Transition note = No longer exists

Again, there is nothing wrong with using terminology but we find that thoughts like, "am I in my chest voice?" or, "am I in my head voice?" or "how do I master my break?" can weigh heavily on a singer's mind. Remember, we don't want you down in the dumps when you practice. If you're worrying about all these things, it could affect your practice and performance.

The only thing you need to focus on is that you have one voice and that the low voice and high voice are connected together through a gear change, which used to be called the vocal *break*. Hum a low note then hum a high note. Feel for the buzz each note creates, and where you feel it in your body. That buzz is your guide and should be your main focus. Now it's time for another assignment.

Assignment #12—Shifting Gears

It's time to slide up and down while humming. Think of the sound an ambulance or a police car makes as it whizzes by with its lights and siren on. The pitch of the siren moves up and down. Our goal is to imitate this sound as we hum. As you begin the hum, use your power, adding more gas as you go higher and less gas as you slide back down again. This doesn't mean you have to get louder. You're using your gas pedal for support so you can make the gear change smoothly.

The secret to a smooth gear change is sliding up slowly so the gear doesn't shift abruptly. After several weeks of practice, the break or "gear change" won't even be noticeable to the listener's ear. Now perform twenty-five hum slides before moving on to the next paragraph. (**Hum Slides**)

Glad to see you made it. Were you able to smooth out the gear change? The more you practice, the smoother it will become. As long as you add downward support, feel the buzz, and experience no strain such as jaw clenching or pain in the throat, you'll do fine. If you feel light-headed once in a while from all the buzzing going on in your head, don't worry. It's proof you're doing something right. In fact, if when focusing on your vocal placement you expand that spinning vibration to vibrate the entire roof of your mouth from the cold spot to the top front teeth, you'll begin feeling stronger vibrations in the mask and effortlessly work through the gear change. If you would commit the following sentence to memory, it will keep you focused on the fluid, flawless voice from the bottom of your range to the top.

More palate buzz equals more mask equals more voice.

Just to recap. Our goal for you is to connect that buzz and make it smooth from the lowest note in your range to the highest. Your transition note should be as smooth as the rest of your voice. The goal in the *Sing Out Loud* exercises is to work toward creating one smooth voice, not two separate voices.

Think of the voice as being in the shape of a cone. A cone is wide at the bottom and narrow and pointy at the top; your low voice is wide at the bottom and narrow and pointy at the top as well. Imagine you are this cone shape from your waist to the top of your head and that you're always filling up the inside of your cone with resonance. At the bottom of the cone the resonance will be heavier, but as it nears the top, the resonance will get lighter because the sides of the cone are narrower. You'll also notice there isn't anywhere inside the cone where resonance can get stuck or flip over a bump because the sides are perfectly smooth.

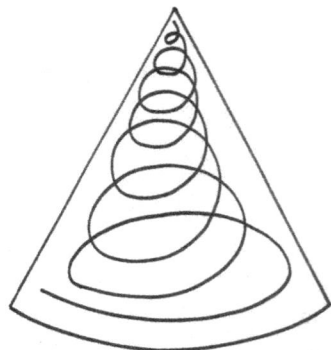

Resonance exists everywhere inside your body because in reality, you are one big tuning fork. And focusing on the tuning fork or cone analogy will help eliminate your break by boosting the resonance. Let's move on to the last lesson chapter where we cover vocal tone. This is where the real fun of exercising the voice begins.

Chapter 9
Adjusting Your Tone

Now that you understand how gear changes can be smoothed to create one full, fluid, flawless voice, let's talk about tuning into different frequencies to vary the tone or color of your voice. You already know you can sound different by singing in falsetto or full voice, and you can even change your vocal color with a high larynx or low larynx to create cartoon-like tones. But there will be times when you want to add more resonance for a bigger sounding tone, or move the resonance around for a lighter, more pleasing effect. Let's jump right into another assignment.

Assignment #13—Tuning Your Tone

It's time to introduce you to different colors by experimenting with a variety of tones. All you need to do is follow along with the audio files as we address the following key points for creating each tone:

- For changes in vocal quality, move the buzz to a different place in your palate (**Moving Palate Buzz**)
- For a smaller sound, add less buzz (**Less buzz/smaller sound**)
- For a bigger sound, add more buzz (**More buzz/bigger sound**)
- For a stronger, thicker tone, move the buzz forward on your palate and feel a strong buzz in the chest (**Thick tone**)
- For a thinner, brighter tone, move the focus of the buzz to the back of the palate towards the cold spot and feel more buzz in the top of the head (**Thin tone**)
- To create a more nasally sound, swallow to raise the larynx, and focus the sensation of the buzz into the sinus cavities by scrunching up your nose (**Nasal tone**)
- For a deep yawning-type tone, yawn more to drop the larynx, keeping the mouth open wide (**Yawning tone**)

The purpose of this assignment is to show you how much the voice can change. But regardless of tonal coloring, the basis of your true tone should be a solid balanced tone that sounds like your speaking voice. You can then change your coloring to suit the mood of the song. Here's a great tip for finding the balanced tone in your real full voice.

Imagine you're swallowing a jawbreaker whole. In other words, open your mouth and raise your palate. This will open up the back of the throat and raise the palate. It will stop you from singing too thin or too "bright" at the top, and too heavy or too "dark" at the bottom. Remember, yawning on the *inhale* was designed to help you create a dome in your mouth, so don't forget to always keep it raised. But don't over-yawn, or you'll end up sounding like a cartoon character. When the palate is raised correctly, it helps bring in the overtones needed to create the perfect tonal mix. It's the same open sensation you feel when you start to sneeze—you take a quick inhale as your nose tickles and you feel the palate and sinuses open up. This open sensation allows tonal freedom. **(The Jaw Breaker)**

Now that your head is filled with enough vocal knowledge to make you dangerous, we'll move into the last chapter of the book, the one you've been waiting for—your brand new workout program. Now the real work begins. Let's get started.

Chapter 10
The Sing Out Loud II Workout

Welcome to your new *Sing Out Loud* vocal workout. This is the time when we put away all the crazy sounds and begin building vocal muscle. This series of vocal scales will function as your vocal warm-up and vocal workout. If you want to improve your voice, you must do this routine five to six days per week before you sing. If you have a band rehearsal, a choir practice, or a gig, you can use the first five exercises for your warm-up. Add more if needed. These scales will wake up your voice and get it prepped for singing.

Warming up the voice is like stretching your leg muscles before running a race. If the voice isn't warmed up, you won't sing your best. This new routine will begin building your vocal muscles for more range and power, while also keeping your voice strong and in shape. It features some old sounds and new exercises. Read the explanations first, and then listen to the audio track.

The following vocal scales will work your voice up and down in range, fine-tune your tones, and build strength and dynamics. You do not have to force yourself to go all the way to the top or all the way to the bottom of each scale. Never strain. Simply stop doing the scale and move on to the next one. Building vocal muscle takes time.

When performing these exercises make sure to focus on your vocal technique. It also helps to stabilize your voice by standing up straight—no slouching. Most of us have a tendency to collapse into the pelvic area, so lift your body up as if it's on a string hooked to the ceiling, like we did in *Sing Out Loud Book I*. If the string visualization doesn't help, you can stand up with your back against the wall to find your posture. Stand erect while bringing the shoulders up parallel. If your shoulders or body begin to slouch, your posture will be out of balance and will make it harder to sing. The next set of pictures shows Abby demonstrating correct and incorrect posture. You can use them as a visual guideline, and then watch yourself in a mirror to correct your own posture.

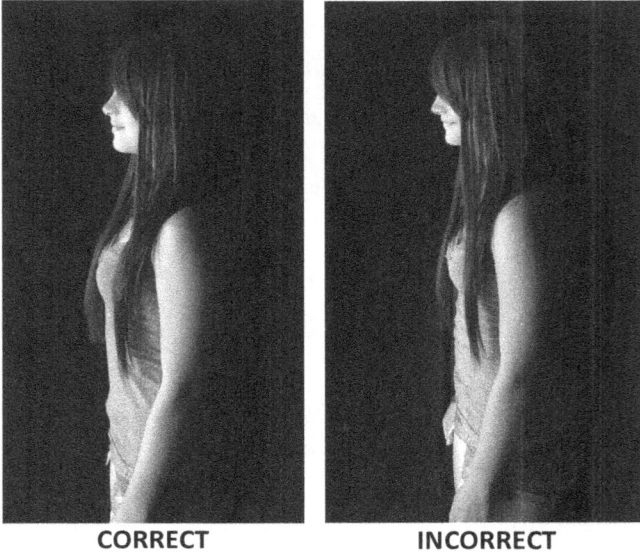

CORRECT   INCORRECT

When you do your vocal workout, always use a mirror so you can make eye contact with yourself during the exercises. Maintaining eye contact will prevent you from looking up for high notes and down for low notes. It will also help in making sure your mouth is open wide enough and you aren't making faces as you sing, which can cause also vocal strain.

Now it's FINALLY time for the exercises. Each exercise has a brief description and accompanying audio track and is best learned by singing along with the audio tracks. Practice the exercises daily and watch your voice become stronger and your tone better.

Exercise 1—Lip Bubbles Walk Down Warm-Up

Follow along with the following example, making sure to use correct technique. By pretending you're saying the word, "**B**ubble", your lip bubbles should sound like a horse blowing through its pursed lips. Most people start lip bubbles as if they are saying the word "**P**uddle", but it's better to start with a "**B**" sound as opposed to a "**P**" sound. That way you won't waste excess breath, or force the production of the sound. The *Sing Out Loud* system requires minimal air to create maximum power. If you start the lip bubble warm-up with a "**B**" sound in as soft a volume as possible, this exercise will help you gain maximum potential. (**Lip Bubbles Walk Down Warm-Up**)

Exercise 2—Mmm Scale Walk Down Warm-Up

You'll perform this scale using the "mmm" sound just like you did in *Sing Out Loud Book I*. The "mmm" sound should make your teeth and cheeks buzz. Feel it in the mask. It's like saying, "mmmmm, that food smells good." (**Mmm Scale Walk Down Warm-Up**)

Exercise 3—Gargling Slide Warm-Up

This exercise sounds a lot like Chewbacca from "Star Wars". It's a great warm-up exercise that makes your vocal cords feel like they're relaxing in a Jacuzzi. Take a swig of water, tilt your head back and make a gargling noise on an "aaah" sound. Hold the sound for a few seconds, and then begin sliding down to the bottom of your range. Be careful not to choke. It may take several attempts before you master this warm-up. Eventually, you want to be able to perform this exercise without that swig of water. Follow the audio demonstration and you'll soon master this exercise. (**Gargling Slide Warm-Up**)

Exercise 4—Falsetto Scale Warm-Up

This is a full scale that requires amazing breath support, but we have the confidence you can do it. (You didn't really think we were going to make it easy at this point, did you?) Just follow along, sing in falsetto on an "E" vowel like in the word "sweet". If you cannot do this exercise on one breath, don't worry because within a few weeks we know you'll be able to master it. (**Falsetto Scale Warm-Up**)

Exercise 5—Light Voice Yah/Yay/Yee/Yo/You Warm-Up

This is the last of the warm-up exercises and should be done in a light voice with minimal volume. Follow the scale, switching from vowel to vowel as demonstrated. If your voice cracks or wobbles as you get higher, stop and take a short break. In time your voice will strengthen enough to allow you to reach the higher notes in the scale. (**Yah/Yay/Yee/Yo/You Warm-Up**)

Exercise 6—Miner Miner Mine

Now we are into your vocal developing exercises. For the remainder of the exercises, you should stay in your full voice. No falsetto allowed. This exercise is a variation of a scale from a program called **Vocal Power** by famed vocal coach Jim Gillette who was known for his amazing vocal range and glass-shattering vocal power. If you want a strong voice, these exercises will get you there. Make sure when you sing the word, "miner", that you add emphasis to the "r" consonant. The scale will be in three parts: "miner-miner-mine". Give each part its due energy. Make sure to end with the "n" on the word "mine". (**Miner Miner Mine Scale**)

Exercise 7—Zee-Lee-Eee-Lee-Mine

This is a variation of another **Vocal Power** scale. Follow along in full voice. As with the last exercise, only go as high as you can comfortably go without straining—work hard, but don't strain. (**Zee-Lee-Eee-Lee-Mine Scale**)

Exercise 8—Do-Re-Mi-Fa-So-La-Ti-Do

This exercise may sound familiar to you because many music teachers have used this to teach beginning students the basic eight-note major scale. Stay in full voice all the way up, and all the way down. As always, breathe with your belly and push down before you sing. (**Do-Re-Mi-Fa-So-La-Ti-Do Scale**)

Exercise 9—Mah-Nah-Wah-Yah

Mah-nah-wah-yah is a fast moving exercise to help work the voice and develop enunciation. Listen closely and try to keep up. (**Mah Nah Wah Yah Scale**)

Exercise 10—Full Voice Yah/Yay Scale

Here's another tough scale. We'll switch between "yah" and "yay". If you need more support to hit the high notes, simply add more downward pressure. (**Full Voice Yah/Yay Scale**)

Exercise 11—The Sabine Power Exercise

As a final muscle engager, we are going to present you with a few exercises from rock star vocal coach and author of the book, *Strengthening Your Singing Voice*, Elizabeth Sabine. Using your entire body, push down and repeat the following:

Go 'way, Go 'way
I Dye, I Dye
Gotta Be, Gotta Be

Use every ounce of your energy to make these sounds. In other words, throw your entire body into it. If done correctly, these three sentences will produce the same sensations as every sound produced in *Sing Out Loud Book I*. **(The Sabine Power Exercise)**

Note: Any time you want to perform the sounds from *Sing Out Loud Book I*, feel free to throw them into your practice schedule, We would suggest, however, that you add them after the Sabine Power Exercises and before your voice cool downs.

Congratulations, we're positive you've done an amazing job with these new exercises. Some of you may be wondering why we haven't discussed vibrato as we promised in *Sing Out Loud Book I*. Vibrato is about adding shine to your singing voice and we'll be addressing that in *Sing Out Loud Book III*. For now just keep focusing on power building and we'll pick back up on vibrato in the next book. Now, let's cool down using the following exercises to help bring the voice back to its normal speaking range.

Exercise 12—Mmm Slide Cool Down

This exercise starts high in pitch on a light resonant "mmm" and then slides down into your lower range. The goal is to start in your high range and work down lower and lower to bring the voice back to a normal speaking tone. When we sing, we increase blood flow to the vocal cords. The cool down exercises help the blood flow return to normal while also relaxing the vocal cords. Keep in mind you can perform your cool downs in falsetto.

Remember to feel the "mmm" buzzing the teeth and cheeks. (**Mmm Slide Cool Down**)

Exercise 13—Lip Bubble Slide Cool Down
This cool down is just like the last cool down, except we're now using lip bubbles. Start high, work low, slide, slide, slide. Make sure to start with a **B** instead of a **P**. (**Lip Bubble Slide Cool Down**)

Great job! That's all there is to strengthening your voice! Now you must begin using your new vocal workout five or six days per week. We know there will be some notes on the exercises you won't be able to reach yet. Don't get frustrated and don't push yourself to reach them or you'll hurt your voice. Singing is a lot like running track. You won't run your best if you don't stretch out and warm-up your legs before the race. It's not only important to "warm-up" the voice before singing, but to also "cool" it down after singing. When you've finished practicing and decide you want to do some singing, we suggest you skip the last two cool down exercises, go right into singing, and then finish with the last two cool downs. After you've done all this, take five minutes for vocal silence. Don't talk to your friends or fans. Use the exercises labeled "warm-up" before your gig, and the exercises labeled "cool down" after your gig.

Each exercise is important so don't cheat and skip one because you don't like it. The ones you hate and find the hardest to conquer are usually the ones that will help you the most. Continual and consistent practice will make the exercises easier within a few months and daily exercises must become a part of a singer's life.

Spend the next four weeks practicing your new routine before moving on to *Sing Out Loud Book III*. Throughout the month, re-read *Sing Out Loud Book II*, making sure you fully understand the vocal techniques. If you have any doubts, you should not move on to *Sing Out Loud Book III*. If you need personal guidance, you can visit www.jaimevendera.com and click on the LESSONS link to schedule an online vocal lesson tailored to your needs. In the meantime, practice all your breathing exercises and the vocal workout and we'll see you in the next series of lessons.

About the Author
Jaime Vendera

Jaime Vendera is the author of a variety of books and one of the most sought-after vocal coaches on the planet. Using the methods he created, Jaime turned his two-octave range into six octaves with massive decibels of raw vocal power that enabled him to set a world record shattering glass with his voice. When singers need more vocal range, power and projection, or need to build up vocal stamina to perform every night, they call Jaime Vendera. Jaime states that, "none of this would have been possible without God."

Ben Thomas of Dweezil Zappa says that Jaime is the 'Mr. Miyagi' of vocal coaches, while Mat Devine of Kill Hannah considers him more of a 'Yoda.' James LaBrie of Dream Theater said, "Because of my lessons with Jaime, my voice is feeling and sounding better than it has in twenty years. I am spot-on every night. He is the Vocal Guru." Myles Kennedy of Alter Bridge said, "One time during a tour, I was so sick I could barely make it through the set. It looked as if we were going to have to cancel the next show. Jaime spent some time giving me some tips that helped me regain my voice. By the next night, I was able to perform the show. He is fantastic! *Raise Your Voice Second Edition* is THE book for singers. I recommend his books and his private instruction to ALL singers." Jaime can be contacted at www.jaimevendera.com.

About the Author
Anne Loader McGee

Anne has studied with a number of well-known Hollywood singing teachers. She has performed in musical theatre productions and taken classes in songwriting, music, and film at both the American Film Institute and the University of California and Los Angeles (UCLA).

She also co-wrote *Strengthening Your Singing Voice* with Elizabeth Sabine, a voice-strengthening expert whom many famous singers, actors, and speakers have consulted over the last twenty-five years. (www.elizabethsabine.net)

As an award winning children's writer, Anne has produced plays for young people, developed animation scripts, and had a number of short stories published in magazines, and in the Los Angeles Times. Anne's middle grade novel, *The Mystery at Marlatt Manor* and *Anni's Attic* are available at Amazon and Barnes & Noble. You can find her at www.annemcgee.com.